I0099530

The Essential Woman

My Secret is Mine, Volume 1

Kristen West McGuire

Published by Secretum Meum Mihi Press, 2023.

THE ESSENTIAL WOMAN

Revised edition, November 30, 2023

Copyright © 2023 Kristen West McGuire.

Print ISBN: 978-0-979-53764-6

Cover art used by permission:

© **St. Edith Stein**, by Br. Claude Lane, OSB, Mount Angel Abbey.

Unless otherwise noted, all scripture citations are from the 1899 Douay-Rheims Bible, public domain.

Excerpts from *Essays on Woman,* by Edith Stein, translated by Freda Mary Oben, (ICS Publications, 1996) used by permission of the publisher.

Table of Contents

For Valencia Burghardt, who rests with the angels now, and who loved like the Samaritan woman, with all her heart...

Preface: St. Teresa Benedicta of the Cross

Edith Stein (St. Teresa Benedicta of the Cross) was born to a Jewish family in 1897 in Breslau, Germany (now Wroclaw, Poland). Academically gifted, she initially pursued psychology but eventually earned a doctorate in philosophy, studying under Edmund Husserl in Gottingen. In 1922, she became a Catholic after reading St. Teresa of Avila's autobiography. She entered the Cologne Carmel in 1934, and was murdered by the Nazis in Auschwitz in 1942. She is the patroness of Secretum Meum Mihi Press. (When her best friend asked why she converted, she was silent but wrote *"secretum meum mihi"* on a nearby paper, which is Latin: *my secret is mine.)*

Stein's public lectures before she became a Carmelite on women's roles in the Church and society were well received and published after her death.

* * *

The following excerpt from "Fundamental Principles of Women's Education," *Essays on Woman*, pp. 132-135 outlines Edith Stein's vision of feminine virtues.

Woman's nature is determined by her original vocation as spouse and mother. One depends on the other. The body of woman is fashioned "to be one flesh" with another and to nurse new human life in itself. A well-disciplined body is an accommodating instrument for the mind which animates it; at the same time, it is a source of power and a habitat for the mind. Just so, woman's soul is designed to be subordinate to man in obedience and support; it is also fashioned to be a shelter in which other souls may unfold. Both spiritual companionship and spiritual motherliness are not limited to the physical spouse and mother relationships, but they extend to all people with whom woman comes into contact.

1

The soul of woman must therefore be expansive and open to all human beings; it must be quiet, so that no small weak flame will be extinguished by stormy winds; warm, so as not to benumb fragile buds; clear, so that no vermin will settle in dark corners and recesses; self-contained, so that no invasions from without can imperil the inner life; empty of itself in order that extraneous life may have room in it; finally, mistress of itself and also of its body, so that the entire person is readily at the disposal of every call.

That is an ideal image of the gestalt of the feminine soul. The soul of the first woman was formed for this purpose, and so, too, was the soul of the Mother of God. In all other women since the fall, there is an embryo of such development, but it needs particular cultivation if it is not to be suffocated among the weeds rankly shooting up around it.

Woman's soul should be expansive, nothing human should be alien to it. Evidently, it has a natural predisposition to such an end: on average, its principal interest is directed to people and to human relations. But, if one leaves the natural instinct to itself, this is expressed in a manner apart from its objective. Often, the interest is chiefly mere curiosity, mere desire to get to know people and their circumstances; sometimes it is real avidity to penetrate alien areas. If this instinct is simply indulged in, then nothing is won either for the soul itself or for other souls. It goes out of itself, so to speak, and remains standing outside of itself. It loses itself, without giving anything to others. This is unfruitful, indeed, even detrimental.

Woman's soul will only profit if it goes abroad to search and to bring home the hidden treasure which rests in every human soul, and which can enrich not only her soul, but also others; and it will profit only if it searches and bears home the well-known or hidden burden which is laid on every human soul. Only the one who stands in wholesome awe before human souls will search in such a manner, one who knows that human souls are the kingdom of God, who knows that one may approach them only if one is sent to them. But whoever is sent will find that which she is seeking, and whoever is so sought will be found and saved. Then the soul does not remain standing on the outside but, on the contrary, carries its booty home; and its expanses must widen in order to be able to take in what it carries.

The soul has to be quiet, for the life which it must protect is timid and speaks only faintly; if the soul itself is in tumult, it will not hear this life which will soon be completely silenced and will disappear from the soul. I wonder whether one can say that the feminine soul is fashioned by nature for this? At first sight, the contrary seems to be true. Women's souls are in commotion so much and so strongly: commotion itself makes much noise; and, in addition, the soul is urged to express its agitation. Nevertheless, the faculty for this quiet must be there; otherwise, it could not be so profoundly practiced as it is, after all, by many women: those women in whom one takes refuge in order to find peace, and who have ears for the softest and most imperceptible little voices.

Woman succeeds if the other requirements are filled: if the soul is empty of self and is self-contained. Indeed when the inherent, agitated self is completely gone, then there is room and quiet to make oneself perceptible to others. But no one can render himself so by nature alone, neither man nor woman. "Oh, Lord God, take me away from myself and give me completely to you alone," the ancient German prayer says. We can do nothing ourselves; God must do it. To speak to Him thus is easier by nature for woman than for man because a natural desire lives in her to give herself completely to someone. When she has once realized that no one other than God is capable of receiving her completely for Himself and that it is sinful theft toward God to give oneself completely to one other than Him, then the surrender is no longer difficult and she becomes free of herself.

Then, it is also self-evident to her to enclose herself in her castle, whereas, before, she was given to the storms which penetrated her from without again and again; and previously she had also gone into the world in order to seek something abroad which might be able to still her hunger. Now, she has all that she needs; she reaches out when she is sent, and opens up only to that which may find admission to her. She is mistress of this castle as the handmaid of her Lord, and she is ready as a handmaid for all whom the Lord desires her to serve. But, above all, this means that she is ready for him who was given to her as a visible sovereign—for her spouse, or also, for those having authority over her in one way or other.

The soul of woman is no doubt warm by nature, but its natural warmth is too seldom constant. It consumes itself and fails when it may be most needed; or it is augmented by a flying spark to the fire which destroys when it should only gently warm. But here again, that can only be helped when, instead of the worldly fire, the heavenly one is known. When the heavenly fire, the divine love, has consumed all impure matters, then it burns in the soul as a quiet flame which not only warms but also illuminates; then all is bright, pure, and clear. Indeed, clarity also does not manifest itself as given by nature. On the contrary, the soul of woman appears dull and dark, opaque to herself and to others. Only the divine light renders it clear and bright.

Thus, everything points to this conclusion: woman can become what she should be in conformity with her primary vocation only when formation through grace accompanies the natural inner formation. Because of this, religious education must be the core of all women's education.

Chapter One: St. Edith Stein...and You

"An evolution which was sensed in advance by some, wanted and worked for by few, and one which surprised most people entirely, has torn women out of the well enclosed realm of the home and out of a matter-of-course kind of life and has suddenly plunged them into the most manifold alien situations and undreamt of problems. We have been thrown into the river, and we must swim. But when our strength threatens to give out, we try to reach at least the shore for safety. We would like to think through the question of WHETHER we should go on; and if we should go on, what should we do so that we will not drown."

—Edith Stein, in "Spirituality of the Christian Woman," *Essays on Woman*

Three quarters of a century after Edith Stein spoke these words to a crowd of Catholic educators, women are no longer conflicted about swimming with the tide. Yet, in the life of nearly every woman I know, there comes a point where she feels she is drowning. There are too many demands on her time, and she senses she is lost in the details of her life. Misunderstood in the workplace, taken for granted by immediate family and overwhelmed by the details of the serious problems around her, modern women face difficult challenges.

I believe Edith Stein experienced many "drowning seasons," often alienated from family members and colleagues, despite deep ties of love and shared responsibility. She saw the women around her with true compassion. They were no strangers to stress, and struggled mightily in an atmosphere that hardly rewarded achievements outside the home. The household work done by her sisters, Rosa and Frieda, enabled the temporal success of her mother's lumber business, her sister Erna's medical work and her own pedagogical endeavors.

Stein delivered the "Essays on Woman" as lectures to teaching conferences between 1928 and 1932. She suggested that women view their natures as two-fold: spouse and mother. This is true whether one is a single lay woman, a wife or a consecrated religious. Either physically or spiritually, a woman is both spouse and mother.

In order to embody the bridal character of the people of God, and to serve as a shelter for souls, Stein suggests that women become expansive, quiet, warm, clear, self-contained, empty (humble) and mistress (self-controlled). The gestalt of these virtues will be unique to each individual. Her aim was to lift up examples that can motivate and comfort women as they strive for wholeness in Christ.

The essays in this book reflect on her idealistic vision of the holy potential of women. I hope they will provide a stable buoy for souls weary of the work and perhaps even fearful of drowning.

Bible Study: Explain "My Secret is Mine"

Isaiah 24:15-18

"Therefore glorify ye the Lord in instruction: the name of the Lord God of Israel in the islands of the sea. From the ends of the earth we have heard praises, the glory of the just one.

And I said: My secret to myself, my secret to myself, woe is me: the prevaricators have prevaricated, and with the prevarication of transgressors they have prevaricated.

Fear, and the pit, and the snare are upon thee, O thou inhabitant of the earth. And it shall come to pass, that he that shall flee from the noise of the fear, shall fall into the pit:

and he that shall rid himself out of the pit, shall be taken in the snare: for the flood-gates from on high are opened, and the foundations of the earth shall be shaken."

Context: This section of the book of Isaiah is known as his Apocalypse. Apocalyptic literature often focused on a future "day of the Lord", when the "just one" would reward the good and punish the bad. In this particular passage, the human praise of the Just One is side by side with His expected wrath to sinners.

Against the bloody backdrop of current Middle East politics, we might be excused for taking the whole section far too grimly to heart. Will the Lord deliver us? Do my secret longings for God's mercy open me up to His justice? Yet, being set free implies the truth that we are imprisoned...spiritually, emotionally, and otherwise.

Translation: Almost certainly, the Bible in your home does not have "my secret is unto me" in it at Isaiah 24:16. Because there are no vowels in Hebrew, a variety of translations are possible, and the context is thus very important. The original Hebrew word, r-z-h, transliterated "ryzyk", translates roughly to "thinness, or leanness". Within the context of the passage, the Latin translation connotes a certainty of weakness as one faces the coming judgment. Subsequent English translations of the original Hebrew use "leanness" - "I waste away," or "I pine away". (Or - I'm skinny! Woe is me!)

Vocabulary

The Just One: a reference to the coming of the Messiah in Jewish apocalyptic literature, who would judge and punish the unrighteous in the last days

Prevaricators: Those who deviate from the truth

The Pit: Hell, or more technically, *Sheol,* a Hebrew concept of the afterlife in which one does not merit God's friendship.

Discussion Questions:

1. Did you get tripped up by the "prevaricators, prevaricating?" It is an alien concept in our culture to call out people who deviate from the truth. Why do you think that is? Is it wise, or not wise, to address someone who "prevaricates?"

2. Edith Stein was ultimately killed at Auschwitz for being Jewish. Religious persecution remains a serious problem today. What should Christians in "safe" countries do to support their suffering and persecuted brothers and sisters in oppressed lands?

3. My secret is mine. Sometimes, I wonder if others even know I am a Christian. As some wag once put it, if the state began to persecute Christians, would they be able to dig up enough dirt to condemn you for the crime? Should we as Catholics proselytize more by words or by example? Why?

Chapter Two: Woman as Spouse
What does it mean to be a Spouse?

Few women today would say that they aspire only to be a good wife. Her successful endeavors might also include motherhood, friendships, a career and household management. Yet, all these goods flow directly from the "spousal" relationship at the center of a woman's vocation, be she single, married or consecrated. Women are uniquely gifted in receiving and giving love, and helping others succeed.

In her 1928 lecture, "The Separate Vocations of Man and Woman According to Nature and Grace," Edith Stein differentiates between the original order created by God in the Garden of Eden, the fallen order after original sin, and the redemptive order instituted by Christ on the cross. It is foundational for women in particular to understand the potential of spousal love within these categories.

In Genesis, both accounts of the creation testify that Adam and Eve are equal in the eyes of the Creator. Their mutual trust flows from God's gift of life, which in turn they give to each other as helpmates. Their shared duty to know, love and serve God reveals that true love is fruitful, giving life.

The serpent in Genesis 3 causes Eve to question her trust in God, and leads both Adam and Eve to disobey God directly. After the fall, their distorted spousal relationship loses the power to become life-giving in all but the carnal sense.

Jesus and Mary take the place of Adam and Eve in the new covenant. The power plays of domination and manipulation are countered by the submission of Mary in the Annunciation and of Jesus in the garden of Gethsemane. Trust in God and in each other is restored by loving obedience which defies worldly logic. In the redemptive order, men and women receive freedom in Christ, not only freedom "from" sin, but the freedom "to" become what we were created by God to be.

For women, Mary is our model of spousal commitment to Christ. This is not an Oedipal complex á la Sigmund Freud, but the exact description of the relationship between Mother and Messiah. Remember that the Annunciation preceded the Nativity. Prior to her exaltation as the mother of God, Mary had to espouse herself, literally, to God the Holy Spirit. Only then could her vocation as mother begin. As the new Eve, Mary's spiritual powers enable all of the temporal duties of her state in life.

You might think, "This is a lovely ideal. But the Church is a mess. Where's the freedom?" Alas, the redemption begun on the cross has yet to be completely fulfilled. We reside temporally between the Cross and the Second Coming. Thus, our personal trust in God and obedience to His promptings is crucial to salvation history. Women have a uniquely prophetic role to play in the Church, as they are intuitively receptive to the Holy Spirit in ways that inspire faith and perseverance in others.

Edith Stein was no ivory tower idealist. She was keenly aware of the dangers and challenges inherent in submitting to male leadership in the temporal order. Women are physically vulnerable, and yet often spiritually stronger. Prophets such as Catherine of Siena and Teresa of Avila convinced Stein, an ardent feminist, that spousal love could be more powerful. Spousal love leads both men and women to submit themselves freely to the promised Kingdom. Seek, and ye shall find.

Bible Study: What does "subordinate" mean?

Ephesians 5:21-28

Be subordinate to one another out of reverence for Christ. Wives should be subordinate to their husbands as to the Lord. For the husband is head of his wife, just as Christ is head of the church, he himself the savior of the body. As the church is subordinate to Christ, so wives should be subordinate to their husbands in everything.

Husbands, love your wives, even as Christ loved the church and handed himself over for her, to sanctify her, cleansing her by the bath of water with the word, that he might present to himself the church in splendor, without spot or wrinkle, or any such thing, that she might be holy and without blemish. So husbands should love their wives as they love their own bodies. He who loves his wife, loves himself. For no one hates his own flesh but rather nourishes and cherishes it, even as Christ does the church, because we are members of his body.

For this reason, a man shall leave [his] father and [his] mother and be joined to his wife, and the two shall become one flesh. This is a great mystery, but I speak in reference to Christ and the church. In any case, each one of you should love his wife as himself, and the wife should respect her husband.

(New American Bible. Excerpts from the Lectionary for Mass for Use in the Dioceses of the United State of America, second typical edition, 2001, Confraternity of Christian Doctrine, Washington, DC. Used with permission. All rights reserved.)

Context: St. Paul is well aware that he is introducing a radical concept here. He models this section after similar household codes in Greco-Roman times that outlined the household relationships. Christianity was (correctly) appraised by some as a challenge to the social order by advocating equality. For this reason, Paul seeks to outline a hierarchical formula in Christian terms. It is fair to say that one might trace the beginning of the modern women's movement all the way back to Paul, who challenges men to lay down their lives for their wives.

Translation: In Colossians 3, one finds a similar listing of the various duties of "inferiors" to their superiors, including the relationship of the slave to his master, and the child to the parent. Experts have noted many structural and verbal similarities between the two books in the original Greek.

Vocabulary:

to be subordinate: The Greek term here (*hupotasso*) has all of the connotations of our own English term. (Obedience to authority of some kind must be a universal linguistic concept.)

without spot or wrinkle: the connotation of the Greek spot (*spilos*) includes a defect or disgrace, and wrinkle (*rhutis*) especially references facial wrinkles.

holy and without blemish: this phrase is a referral back to the Old Testament concept of being chosen, and the chosen people of God.

respect: The Greek term (*phobeo*) is more directly translated as "fear", or, perhaps, awe and reverence.

Few married men today insist that their wives must obey them. At the same time, it is clear from the success of pop culture psychologists like Dr. Phil that relations between the sexes haven't evolved much past the original apple bite that broke the harmony of Eden.

The first lines of this scripture intrigue me, in juxtaposition with the last line. Essentially, Paul is pointing out that leaders endure a passion all their own. As too many evangelical pastors have found out the hard way, he who exalts himself is humbled. Women have good reasons to fear, even and especially in the #MeToo era.

We each belong to the Lord in varying degrees of justice and mercy. The mutual submission of married life is not a blind one, but entirely focused on the good God who needs us to be His hands and feet in the world. Leaders lead by example. If we wish others to submit (or respect), we must model our own submission (and honor) to God first, and to others in service second. It is indeed a mystery...but a very powerful tool to build the Kingdom.

Discussion Questions:

1. Do you think St Paul had a realistic vision of the possibilities of married life? Why or Why not?

2. When St Paul instructs the father to "lay down his life" for the sake of the wife and the children, what does he mean? What are some concrete examples of this idea?

3. In an abusive or dysfunctional relationship, how does the injunction to "fear" one's husband translate? How would you encourage and strengthen a woman facing such evil?

Chapter Three: Spiritual Motherhood
I am a Shelter for Souls?

Like many young brides, I welcomed the opportunity to create a more beautiful space when I married a man with a wagon wheel couch and a crate style dinette. It's fun to decorate and to make spaces for work, play and rest. Especially during those (long) years that I sat nursing an infant and watching my toddlers play, I was constantly re-decorating the room in my mind for health, safety and aesthetic reasons.

But it can become a mania, too. Can't it?

And yet, by the time we move out of the home, perhaps years later, we are only too aware of the many deficits of the abode. We know which knobs are loose, which drains clog easily and the exact right way to run the appliances so they don't break. We can hardly wait to move. The shelter that we invested so much creativity into devolves in our memories to a list of projects.

Until we move. Each time I have walked out and shut the door behind me, driving off to a new shelter, I have cried. And each child who has grown and flown the nest leaves my heart in tatters.

As I did to my own mother before me, and hers before that. A long line of homes that we leave, to embrace a new home. The mother's heart is the guardian of those memories. The shelter she provides is in her soul. And the homes we create are for one another.

When Edith Stein decided to pursue a semester of graduate work in Gottingen, with Dr. Edmund Husserl, her mother agreed, but was clearly dreading her departure. At the time, Edith assured her it was only a semester. But, as she recalled later, both mother and daughter knew in their hearts it would likely be a permanent move. She would have to leave the nest and fly solo to fulfill her vocation.

Frau Stein surely cried when Edith left.

There is a light that shines in a mother's eyes when she sees her adult children after a long absence. It shines from deep within. And we can, and do, create space for the souls of friends, of colleagues, of employees, of children. Women have a unique capacity for creating a warm and inviting place where others may enter in and find rest.

Edith Stein calls this, "being a shelter for souls."

The simple act of offering a gentle smile, a peaceful demeanor, a listening ear, a place to rest, is motherhood, if only for a few minutes. The recipients know they've touched upon a secret, the divine Secret, within. This is a beautiful reality— creating a safe space where our beloved friends and family can unfold.

The light of God radiates through a woman when she embraces spiritual maternity. We can even see it in a prophetic sense, that we create on earth this safe space for one another. As souls draw strength, the motherly heart rejoices.

Stein experienced this shelter in her home, and later lived it as the teacher in a high school for girls. Dr. Stein taught her students to carry out the sometimes monotonous and even difficult tasks of daily life. And, with her entry into Carmel, and even in her martyrdom, she continually was a witness to the power of love to transform lives.

This is part of the unique contribution that we can make as women in the "public arena," as Stein says. At home or in the office, women welcome and nurture the souls entrusted to us. The secret of providing shelter is to remember that our eternal home is the one each one of us is called to. Heaven is our true home, and the shelter we find on earth is just a foretaste of that truth.

Bible Study: She Shall be Saved by Childbearing

I Timothy 2:8-15

I will therefore that men pray in every place, lifting up pure hands, without anger and contention. In like manner women also in decent apparel: adorning themselves with modesty and sobriety, not with plaited hair, or gold, or pearls, or costly attire, But as it becometh women professing godliness, with good works.

Let the woman learn in silence, with all subjection. But I suffer not a woman to teach, nor to use authority over the man: but to be in silence. For Adam was first formed; then Eve. And Adam was not seduced; but the woman being seduced, was in the transgression. Yet she shall be saved through childbearing; if she continues in faith, and love, and sanctification, with sobriety.

Context: The entire first chapter of I Timothy outlines concerns in Ephesus regarding false teaching. Paul tells Timothy to remain there and root out false doctrine. The dominant goddess among pagans in Ephesus was Artemis, sister of Apollo and goddess of childbirth. The Temple of Artemis of the Ephesians was understood to provide prosperity—the Temple itself received "donations" in such a way that it served as an informal bank by our standards. There is no evidence that the rituals practiced to honor Artemis were sexual, rather, the virtue of virginity was celebrated. So, the false doctrines in Ephesus disdained marriage and childbirth, and also led to disputations in worship that did not honor God.

Translation: This passage of scripture continues to spark fierce debates in modern Protestant faith communities. The Catholic Church is one of the few still refusing to ordain women to the priesthood, based on both scripture and the consistent prohibition of the early Church fathers. My observation is that in the Protestant churches, there is no role for women outside of clerical roles, whereas in the Catholic Church, there are role models such as consecrated virgins, inspiring religious sisters and holy women saints and martyrs to emulate.

Vocabulary:

Saved sṓzō (Greek, from *sōs,* "safe, rescued") – to deliver out of danger and into safety; used principally of God rescuing believers from the penalty and power of sin –and into His provisions (safety).

Childbearing teknogonía This is the only instance in the entire Bible of this Greek term for "childbearing." In other places, the word *egkuos* is used, which means, "with child" or "pregnant." The connotation of *teknogonía* expands beyond giving birth and extends to parenting the child to adulthood.

Sobriety sóphrosuné: This term means soundness of mind, and connotes self-control. It also clearly points to sobriety.

I don't know about you, but I have had multiple experiences over my lifetime of women sharing their insights on the gospel in a way that challenged my presuppositions and realigned my priorities. Sometimes, I didn't care for the way I was told a particular nugget of golden wisdom. However, later, I reflected and embraced what was clearly a call from God for me to repent, and learn.

How does God save us? Well, yes, he died on the cross to save us from our sins. But in the rough and tumble of daily life, it is often His prophets—the women who proclaim the Gospel loudly by their lives—who inspire conversions and even transformations of entire nations. (Think about St. Joan of Arc, or St. Helena of the Cross.) While having lots of babies is certainly laudable, "through child bearing" can also be seen as having the spiritual discipline to lead, teach and correct souls, informally and with powerful prayers.

Jesus gave His own mother to us on the cross, through the beloved Disciple. As women, we find ourselves thrust in roles that defy hierarchy and influence many more people than we expected. How can "childbearing" become a prayer for bringing all Christians into the safety and provision of God?

Discussion Questions:

1. Have you ever struggled with the meaning of childbearing in your life? Is it a welcome gift? Has childbearing included many sacrifices for you? Have you not been able to have children despite yearning for motherhood? Sometimes we inadvertently make things harder for women in a parish by focusing too much on the "obvious" maternity of physical pregnancy. How can we talk about maternity in our church with greater sensitivity to all women?

2. What saints or religious sisters have brought meaning into your life? How have you experienced their spiritual maternity?

3. Self-control and sobriety can be difficult to practice in our larger culture that celebrates excess and material comforts. What practices of quiet asceticism work for you?

Chapter Four: Expansiveness
Edith Stein's Love Unto the Cross

When telling a story, who wants to know all the juicy details? It's a stereotype, but the majority of men I know are satisfied with the barest of facts. Meanwhile, women seek to know the nuance of every player in the room. Left unchecked, this kind of attention to others can turn into a kind of spiritual prison for a woman, enslaved to the latest gossip, forever roving outside of her own legitimate concerns.

However, when the drive to reach outside of oneself and "know" another soul is harnessed with prudence and faith, that very expansiveness is the root of the evangelization of all peoples, through the intercession of the Blessed Mother herself.

How does one tell the difference between idle curiosity and evangelization? Ye shall know them by their fruits (cf. Luke 6:43-45). When one is sent by the Spirit, the soul receives "hidden treasure" from that other soul, which in turn enlarges its capacity to love and sacrifice for the sake of love. You can know you were "sent" by the Spirit when the fruit of your work adds to your holiness.

Edith Stein's decision to enter Carmel bears striking testimony to her expansiveness. On the first Friday in April, 1900 years after the death of Jesus on the cross, Stein was at a momentous crossroads. With the Third Reich firmly in charge, she already guessed she would be barred from instruction because of her Jewish ancestry.

What was she to do?

Stein spent her adult years fighting for the right of women to teach at a university. She had finally reached that goal in 1932, albeit for a girl's college! A college in South America offered her a job, but she could not bring herself to leave the country she loved. She considered anew her desire to become a Carmelite nun.

She later wrote of her extraordinary prayers from that Triduum in 1933:

> *"I talked with the Saviour and told Him that I knew that it was His cross that was now being placed on the Jewish people; that most of them did not understand this, but that those who did would have to take it up willingly in the name of all. I would do that."* ("How I Came to the Cologne Carmel" in Edith Stein: Selected Writings, translated by Susanne Batzdorff, Templegate 1990, p. 17)

Indeed, her own mother was devastated by her decision, as Edith knew she would be. All her relatives strongly felt that she was abandoning them in their hour of direst need. Yet, she knew she shared their fate.

At the time, she had only vague premonitions of impending doom. She told her niece that Carmel would be unable to protect her from her fate as a Jew. She told her students that the sins of Germany would have to be atoned for as well. She would do that.

Her sacrificial love is a mystery I am not sure I understand in a rational way. It is the secret of the cross of Jesus that I do not fully share yet. I am repelled by the evils of Nazi Germany, and repelled by evils that continue to this day. And yet, it is impossible to ignore the sanctity that Stein attained in her mission. So, expansiveness includes hidden burdens which enlarge the soul, even as it contains hidden treasure.

My treasure seeking seems a rather puny endeavor compared to the huge stakes of Edith Stein's undertaking. Haphazardly seeking the "booty" hidden in souls around me, I probably miss many opportunities to be sent, and alternatively foist myself as a burden to others at inopportune moments. But on those occasions when I get it right, when my soul expands to feed on the treasure I have received, I resolve anew to be ready, and to be sent, as often as my sweet Savior calls me.

Bible Study: The Women at the Foot of the Cross

John 19:25-27

Now there stood by the cross of Jesus, his mother, and his mother's sister, Mary of Cleophas, and Mary Magdalen. When Jesus therefore had seen his mother and the disciple standing whom he loved, he saith to his mother: Woman, behold thy son. After that, he saith to the disciple: Behold thy mother. And from that hour, the disciple took her to his own.

In lieu of notes on context, translation and vocabulary, the following is a synopsis by Kristen West McGuire of a commentary on this section of the book of John by Adrienne von Speyr, a Swiss mystic and doctor of the mid-20th century. (*The Birth of the Church: Meditations on John 18-21[1]*. Vol. 4. Translated by David Kipp. San Francisco: Ignatius Press, 1991.)

Alongside John, the beloved disciple, there are three women at the foot of the cross. Mary, the mother, personifies the suffering of the righteous. Conversely, the Magdalene personifies the sinners for whom Jesus dies. The wife of Cleophas in the middle gives roundness to the reality that Jesus died for all of us, even the garden variety Catholic woman. Von Speyr reminds us that "one need be neither exceptionally pure, nor exceptionally sinful in order to be looked upon in a special way by the Lord at the cross." Thus, we should never assume that our most ordinary of days nor mundane duties keep us from salvation.

Many humble, quiet days of work in the home separated Nazareth from Golgotha for Mary. From the moment of the Annunciation, Mary was the "potential" mother, just as Jesus in the womb was the "potential" Redeemer. When potential turned to reality, Jesus the divine Redeemer bequeathed divine Motherhood upon his mother. "...fruitful Christian motherhood," exhorts von Speyr, "...lives as joy in self-sacrificing devotedness."

1. *https://ignatius.com/john-vol-4-j4h/*

We are the recipients of her devotion now. "Bodily fruitfulness requires overseeing the fruit," finishes von Speyr. Conversely, "Fruitfulness in the Lord requires giving up all claim to overseeing one's life." Her obedience is intertwined in ours.

Mary's obedience helps us aspire to eternal salvation. The grace which opened the gates of heaven to all men makes Jesus our brother, and thus His Mother our mother. Like so many Christians, I received Mary in darkness, barely aware of her intercession at first. Her obedience mysteriously enables my own.

What about John? Jesus' bond with John is not like intimacy as many of us live it. Love for Jesus is expansive and open; not limited to those within its hold, and impossible to keep within. Whatever we receive of Jesus' love is meant to be shared, not the extra, but all that we receive. As Jesus shares His love with John, it exponentially expands to the disciples and beyond, even to us here in the present.

Jesus gives his mother to John in the same virginal love that she bore Him in Bethlehem. It is a pure love that reflects directly the loving gaze of the Father in obedience and submission. Where others may look upon the virginal love and see only renunciation and hardship, its divine counterpart is unlimited fruitfulness. Mary receives us, nurtures us, and returns us to God the Father in love. Our fruit is her Fruit.

Discussion Questions:

1. Pretend to be John. You are to take the Blessed Virgin into your home to care for her. Yet, she will also care for you. What gifts can you offer her? What gifts might she offer to you?

2. Three women named Mary are at the foot of the cross during the passion – the Blessed Virgin suffering, the wife of Cleophas present, the sinner Magdalene grateful – which one are you?

3. All love we offer each other is borrowed from God. Does that idea make it easier to love, or more overwhelming?

Chapter Five: Quiet
The Joy Edith Found in Silence

Some say women problem solve by talking through the cascade of their thoughts. It works for me. But middle age has slowed my spigot. Perhaps it's maturity, or multiple problems to solve, or memories of young mouths calling for "mom" 200 times a day, but I have come to appreciate a little silence.

Edith Stein was middle-aged when she entered the novitiate in October 1933. It was a joyful move for her, despite the sadness of her family in the background. Obediently bowing herself to the rigors of the Carmelite rule was a freeing experience, especially the silence. In fact, Sr. Teresia Posselt, her novice-mistress at the Cologne Carmel, remembered, "It was sheer joy to observe her growing younger and more radiant after her first weeks in the enclosure...needing only to be like a child among children."

Silence isn't only found in the cloister. While there's a time and a place for prayerful ecstasies, most of us need a little quiet to receive the Word of the Lord. Silence allows God a place to enter into conversation. And, it provides a counter-balance to the Babel of the modern workday.

Edith Stein believed all women were both capable and called to cultivate interior silence. The faculty of quiet is a summons to the soul, a receptivity to the divine that allows us to become what we are – beloved of God.

After entering the novitiate, the happy postulant wrote to her friend, Sr. Adelgundis Jaegerschmid, OSB:

"Most of the sisters consider it a penance to be called to the speakroom. It is, after all, like a transition into a strange world, and we are happy to flee once more into the silence of the choir and, before the Tabernacle, to ponder over those matters which have been entrusted to us. But I still regard this peace, daily, as an immense gift of grace that has not been given for one's own exclusive benefit. And when someone comes to us worn out and crushed, and then takes away a bit of rest and comfort, it makes me very happy."

Look for the small comforts we can offer ourselves and others by forming a refuge of silence within our hearts. Pondering the needs of our lives in the stillness, we will find the solutions we seek and the strength to follow through with the answers. The gentle peace of our Savior is given to us for sharing.

Bible Study: Martha and Mary

Luke 10:38-42

"Now it came to pass as they went, that he entered into a certain town: and a certain woman named Martha, received him into her house. And she had a sister called Mary, who sitting also at the Lord's feet, heard his word. But Martha was busy about much serving. Who stood and said: Lord, hast thou no care that my sister hath left me alone to serve? speak to her therefore, that she help me. And the Lord answering, said to her: Martha, Martha, thou art careful, and art troubled about many things: But one thing is necessary. Mary hath chosen the best part, which shall not be taken away from her. "

Context: A simple, common meal in biblical times was not a matter of running to the corner grocer. The wheat or barley kernels had to be ground first, usually with a stone hand mill, wielded by experienced feminine hands. It takes an hour of grinding to make enough for two loaves of bread. The bread dough was kneaded and patted into flat loaves, and baked on a hot stone, or in a clay baker.

Ordinarily, dessert would have just been fruit, but it is likely Martha hoped for something less mundane. Perhaps she thought to stuff the dates with nuts or sweet meats, or to grind the flour extra fine and add nuts and honey to little wafers. The beverage was wine, which was mixed with water. (And who would go to the well for the water?)

Translation: This story pops up only in the Gospel of Luke. Luke never overlooks the forgotten work of those the history books mention least. At the same time, Jesus teaches the disciples how to pray the "Our Father" prayer in the next section. So, consider how Luke is juxtaposing an important message for women about prayer here.

The story does not indicate that any men were lurking nearby, worried that Martha was working too hard. Within traditional Jewish gender roles, men prayed and studied the Torah to express their faith, while women expressed their faith by keeping a kosher home and serving them with love. So, in Martha's eyes, her hospitality was her way of expressing her love for Jesus.

The phrase "one thing is needful" might also be translated, "few things are needful," implying that Martha might have been piling on the hospitality a little too thickly. Either way, it seems clear that Jesus is proposing a sea change in the way that women expressed their faith.

Vocabulary:

distracted The King James version renders the Greek *perispao* as "cumbered." This is a figurative way of expressing Martha's work load dragging along behind her.

serving The Greek *diakoneia* here is explicitly used in other places to describe the good works of the ministry of the Church, and her deacons who served the poor.

portion This word is *meris*, a feminine version of a similar term for men's portion. It also connotes participation.

For most of my life, I have "sided" with Martha over Mary. Jesus' response to Martha seemed harsh and unfair. Once the kids came along, I decided Martha really got a bad rap. Dreams of beautiful dinner parties faded under the weight of getting each meal cleaned up before the next one. Somebody's got to get the chow on the table, Jesus!

My empathy with poor Martha masked a deeper issue. Often, I lost my temper with my husband and my children. In the confessional, gradually, I was shocked to discover a little scoreboard in my head. All through the days, weeks, months, and years, I had been keeping score. And was I ever a martyr— just like Martha!

Too often, women will offer their busy-ness to the Lord when, in reality, His priorities may be deeper...or even different. The work of our vocation may become an idol, especially meal preparation. The point is that God comes first. When we truly serve Him first, seeking the Kingdom in all we do, we will find that there is time enough to praise Him and to accomplish the "needful" things. First we receive His love, and then we sling that hash.

Mary chose the better portion, to sit at Jesus' feet and trust that the necessary work would happen. If it had been her divine duty to help, wouldn't Jesus have told her to help? But He did not. Did Jesus love Martha less because she shouldered a heavier household burden? No! But he invited her to place her anxieties upon his altar, and pick up only the ones Jesus expected her to carry. No fancy table linens. Appetizers optional. Plain figs for dessert.

Discussion Questions:

1. What busy-ness on your calendar needs to be placed at Jesus' feet? How might you begin to whittle down your "to-do" list?

2. Is there a scoreboard problem at your house? What would it take to disable it?

3. Sometimes, there is a certain satisfaction in doing housework that is a respite from the harder work of interacting with people, even our loved ones. What housework is your refuge, and why?

Chapter Six: Warmth
Cleaning Me With Fire

In the Methodist church of my youth, I loved singing in the folk choir. One year, we performed a cantata based on the Catholic Order of the Mass. (Liturgical purists are absolved for raising their eyebrows at this point.)

The chorus of the Confiteor (the "confession" prayer just before the Gloria) still rings in my head: "Cleaning me with fire, that is my desire, burning me up, consuming my whole heart, 'til it's all aflame!" The chasm that existed between my sins and the consuming fire was large, but my desire for such a cleansing was kindled.

Many years later, I reluctantly scheduled my "first confession," convinced it was an unnecessary condition for receiving my first Eucharist. Why did I need to purify myself? Wasn't it enough that Jesus already knew my sins, and died on the cross to set me free?

I thought, "Those repetitive Catholics, keeping guilt nipping at their heels, hiding their sins behind the velvet curtains, mumbling a few Hail Marys." Confession seemed like a therapeutic end-run on Jesus' mercy. Grumbling, I pulled back the veil. There I sat, warts and all.

I changed my mind after one confession. The patient priest helped me realize that mercy was a long-term project. A one-time bonfire was too scary, but I could handle a regular application of penitential singes, in and out of the confessional. When the fire burns too brightly, it is hard to see what God might want through all the smoke.

Dr. Edith Stein served as Dr. Edmund Husserl's postdoctoral assistant in 1917-18. Although she competently organized his notes and taught an introductory philosophy course, Husserl rebuffed her attempts to be a colleague, and refused to sponsor her for a university professorship. Finally, she quit. Although she remained cordial with Husserl, her closest friends were aware of her pain and disappointment over the situation.

In 1932, a friend visited the elderly master, and wrote to Edith that she had conversed with him about the "last things" (death, judgment, heaven, hell). Edith chided her against such attempts at influencing the souls of others, saying, "...doing so heightens his responsibility as well as our responsibility for him...After every encounter in which I am made aware how powerless we are to exercise direct influence, I have a deeper sense of the urgency of my own *holocaustum*."

What haunting words! Though she could not have known what terror the future held for her at the time, her wisdom in spite of her past pain proves her sanctity. Humility keeps us rightly focused on our own transformation.

Repentance and conversion involve fires which must be tended by our Savior himself. Fires on earth are deadly business. May God help us be truly wise in his service.

Bible Study: Queen Esther Gets the Job Done

Esther 7:1-10

So the king and Haman went in to feast with Queen Esther. And on the second day, as they were drinking wine, the king again said to Esther, "What is your petition, Queen Esther? It shall be granted you. And what is your request? Even to the half of my kingdom, it shall be fulfilled."

Then Queen Esther answered, "If I have found favor in your sight, O king, and if it please the king, let my life be given me at my petition, and my people at my request. For we are sold, I and my people, to be destroyed, to be slain, and to be annihilated. If we had been sold merely as slaves, men and women, I would have held my peace; for our affliction is not to be compared with the loss to the king."

Then King Ahasu-erus said to Queen Esther, "Who is he, and where is he, that would presume to do this?" And Esther said, "A foe and enemy! This wicked Haman!" Then Haman was in terror before the king and the queen. And the king rose from the feast in wrath and went into the palace garden; but Haman stayed to beg his life from Queen Esther, for he saw that evil was determined against him by the king. And the king returned from the palace garden to the place where they were drinking wine, as Haman was falling on the couch where Esther was; and the king said, "Will he even assault the queen in my presence, in my own house?" As the words left the mouth of the king, they covered Haman's face.

Then said Harbona, one of the eunuchs in attendance on the king, "Moreover, the gallows which Haman has prepared for Mordecai, whose word saved the king, is standing in Haman's house, fifty cubits high." And the king said, "Hang him on that." So they hanged Haman on the gallows which he had prepared for Mordecai. Then the anger of the king abated.

Context: The Book of Esther is an apologetical work, explaining the Jewish feast of Purim. While some historians hold that the book dates from the second century B.C. at the earliest, it recounts the deliverance of the Jewish people from a fifth century B.C. pogrom attempted by the Persians.

Esther risks her life to mediate with the King in the face of persecution of her people by his minister Haman. The snippet at left tells only the ending; the entire story includes the details of how the Jewess Esther happened to become the queen, and the way in which Mordecai had already proven his worthiness to the king.

Translation: This book does not mention God even once, a trait it shares with the Song of Songs. Over the centuries, both Christian and Jewish scholars have debated its accuracy for this reason and others. However, the popularity of the story among Jews and its consistent appearance among canonical texts argues for its authenticity. (Even the famous Jewish scholar Maimonides called the book of Esther second only to the Torah.) Besides, the inclusion of a brave and intelligent woman's story in the Bible is surely a gift of God in the first place.

Jews call this scripture the *Megillat,* and the story of Esther is read (either at home or in the synagogue) on Purim, replete with booing, hissing and noisemakers. Some exhort one another to drink enough that one cannot differentiate between "cursed be Haman" and "blessed be Mordecai." That might be why Americans refer to this holiday as the Jewish Mardi Gras.

Vocabulary:

feast The word feast in the first verse of chapter seven, *shahthah,* emphasizes the alcoholic content of the festive menu. All the other references to feasts in the book of Esther use the word *mishteh,* which derives from the same root, but emphasizes the banquet.

assault Did the king think Haman and Esther were having a lover's quarrel? Or did he think Esther was about to be raped? The Hebrew word *kabash*, meaning to force or to be subjugated, connotes the latter interpretation.

cubits A cubit was a measurement of the distance between the tip of the middle finger to the elbow (the length of the forearm). Understandably, the length of a standard cubit varied among the cultures of the ancient near east.

Esther is a heroine worth emulating. The Bible does not say if she was an observant Jew, mentioning neither the kosher laws nor even the prayers common to the Jewish woman. Still, Esther got the job done. Sometimes, a focus on outward piety can sometimes get in the way of legitimate work.

Esther knew that execution was the punishment for daring to appear before the king without request. She prepared herself for the dangerous mission by fasting. Even if the book of Esther doesn't mention prayer, fasting is closely related to it. Meanwhile, the feast would have required her time and attention, as would her attire and toilette after the fast. We have some serious penance going on in preparation for her big ask. (Be honest! Isn't preparing for a party, and dressing up to impress a lot of work?)

Esther's genius is shown in her forethought about what the king might appreciate about her. She presents herself in beauty, and invites him to feast with more than his eyes. And, when the first feast was done, wouldn't you want to be done also? But, wisely, she merely asks for the favor of a second round of serious hospitality. Esther earned her people's redemption, no doubt about it. When a religious person offers a sincere gift of self, only illogical antipathy rejects the gesture. Boo, hiss, Haman! Esther defeated you with honor!

Discussion Questions:

1. Then as now, drinking alcohol can predispose someone to think kindly on your plans. Have you ever poured an extra glass for a man in hopes of getting him to see things your way? Do you regret it? Why or why not?

2. Esther was careful to express her warmth and respect for the king tangibly before making her good faith request. Is it ever possible to secure true justice quickly? Are women better than men in visualizing the possibilities for justice? What could that mean for world peace?

3. Have you ever been a witness to injustice coming to light? Can we as Christians do more to uncover evil?

Chapter Seven: Clarity
Clearing the Vermin from Dark Corners

"When the heavenly fire, the divine love, has consumed all impure matters, then it burns in the soul as a quiet flame which not only warms but also illuminates; then all is bright, pure, and clear. Indeed, clarity also does not manifest itself as given by nature. On the contrary, the soul of woman appears dull and dark, opaque to herself and to others. Only the divine light renders it clear and bright." –Edith Stein, "Fundamental Principles of Women's Education", in Essays on Woman, p. 135.

Before Edith Stein left Breslau for Gottingen in 1913, one of her fellow students remarked to her, "Well, I wish you the good fortune of finding in Gottingen people who will satisfy your taste. Here you seem to have become far too critical." Edith was dumbstruck. She had assumed that people thought well of her, and that her tendency to mock the faults of others was well-received. Apparently, it wasn't.

She reflected later, "I had been living in the naïve conviction that I was perfect...I was not angry with him for saying [these words]. Nor did I shrug them off as an undeserved reproach. They were for me a first alert to which I gave much reflection." (Life in a Jewish Family, p. 195-6) The dark corners of our hearts, minds and souls are often a surprise even to ourselves.

Whereas in the last essay we talked about the passion of God's love burning out the impurities in our souls, now we turn to the aftereffects of such cleansing. The divine flame now burns in a cleared area in the soul, and it is easier to assess the darker outlines of our deeds that are tainted by self-interest and pride, rather than a love that continually is renewed by sacrificial self-giving.

Sometimes it makes us angry when others reveal these "minor" faults to us, such as Edith's excessive honesty. After all, most of us are doing the best that we can, and this isn't heaven. There are so many problems, and sometimes our advice is objectively good. Is it wrong to offer advice, even if it is self-righteous in tone?

Without realizing it, Edith Stein imitated the Blessed Mother in this episode of her life. She pondered the hurtful words, applying them to her actions, and seeking to live a deeper Truth. God is the housekeeper of the soul. He clears the corners for us. All we have to do is ponder, in the quiet light of truth, all that we might ask Him to sweep away for the sake of our salvation.

Bible Study: Washing His Feet with Her Tears

Luke 7: 36-50

And one of the Pharisees desired him to eat with him. And he went into the house of the Pharisee, and sat down to meat. And behold a woman that was in the city, a sinner, when she knew that he sat at meat in the Pharisee's house, brought an alabaster box of ointment; And standing behind at his feet, she began to wash his feet, with tears, and wiped them with the hairs of her head, and kissed his feet, and anointed them with the ointment. And the Pharisee, who had invited him, seeing it, spoke within himself, saying: This man, if he were a prophet, would know surely who and what manner of woman this is that toucheth him, that she is a sinner. And Jesus answering, said to him: Simon, I have somewhat to say to thee. But he said: Master, say it.

A certain creditor had two debtors, the one who owed five hundred pence, and the other fifty. And whereas they had not wherewith to pay, he forgave them both. Which therefore of the two loveth him most? Simon answering, said: I suppose that he to whom he forgave most. And he said to him: Thou hast judged rightly. And turning to the woman, he said unto Simon: Dost thou see this woman? I entered into thy house, thou gavest me no water for my feet; but she with tears hath washed my feet, and with her hairs hath wiped them. Thou gavest me no kiss; but she, since she came in, hath not ceased to kiss my feet.

My head with oil thou didst not anoint; but she with ointment hath anointed my feet. Wherefore I say to thee: Many sins are forgiven her, because she hath loved much. But to whom less is forgiven, he loveth less. And he said to her: Thy sins are forgiven thee. And they that sat at meat with him began to say within themselves: Who is this that forgiveth sins also? And he said to the woman: Thy faith hath made thee safe, go in peace.

Context: This invitation to dinner came to Jesus against a backdrop of increasing tension. The Pharisees demanded ritual purity of their dinner guests. So, while Jesus was accused of dining with tax collectors and sinners, it is clear the Pharisees considered him at least worthy of their table.

Large feasts were open to the public in biblical times, and the poor could enter, listen and eat, so long as they were not disruptive. So, the presence of the woman at the table would not have been noticed before she began to weep. Only slaves cleaned feet; the sinful woman may have been poor, but she was not a slave!

When the woman begins to use her hair to dry his feet, the scandalized dinner guests must have been in shock. One's tresses were never let loose in public, and to use one's hair as a tool was a deep social embarrassment, both for her and for Jesus, who accepts her gesture.

Translation: This story in the book of Luke appears after several encounters with the Pharisees and general teachers of Judaic law. Two more banquet conflict stories are found in the book of Luke, in verses 11:37 and 14:1. This first account presents Jesus as the prophet of mercy.

Luke draws the reader in by presenting the salacious details first. The host has omitted certain customary courtesies toward Jesus, but we don't learn of this oversight until after the parable of the creditors. A first century Greek reader would have been shocked at the heedless actions of the woman, but then disappointed at the self-centered reaction of Simon the Pharisee.

Vocabulary:

sinner: The Greek word *amarantos* has the connotation of misdeeds that do not fade away. Once one had "missed the mark" in this society, public opinion registered the negative verdict, often permanently. Likely the woman felt she had nothing to lose.

Master: The Pharisee calls Jesus *"didaskalos"* which was an ambiguous title (rendered in other translations as Teacher) indicative of his disregard, a subtle put-down.

loved much...loveth less: The Greek in this passage *(agape)* means love in the social or moral sense, implying an assent of the will. There is another Greek term for love, *phileo,* which connotes personal attachment and affection. It is the deep *agape* love, heedless of consequences, that Jesus highlights.

Many scholars have debated the identity and putative sins of this nameless woman in Luke 7:36-50. Does it matter who this sinner was? Does it change the quality of her repentance to know the details of her sins? Once her heart discovered the truth about Jesus, and she recognized his power to forgive her sins, she fell to the floor in gratitude and joy.

During Holy Week and the Easter season, I challenge myself to join her on the floor, and to weep with gratitude for the gifts of mercy that He brings to my life. Who is this, who even forgives sins? This is Jesus, and He has offered to forgive everything and make us new in the fire of His Passion. As Lent turns to Easter, may we find anew the saving power of His forgiveness, every day.

Discussion Questions:

1. Have you ever done something so shocking that a room fell silent? If so, how does that experience affect your reading of this gospel? If not, does it bother you when others flaunt social conventions?

2. Have you ever befriended a social misfit? Does this story prompt any ideas about doing so in the future? Why or why not?

3. Have you ever worried that your sins have placed you beyond the mercy of even God? According to Luke, it is not our sins, but our lack of repentance that hardens our hearts. What freedom does Jesus offer to you in this story?

Chapter Eight: Stability
Weathering the Storms of Life

"How do you do it all?" Strangers and friends alike point to my eight children and bursting day planner with skeptical eyebrows. Many days, I'm not sure! My husband hands out the oars each morning, and the whole family rows (mostly in synch). Somehow, the "U.S.S. McGuire" makes it back to port each night.

When the going was rougher several years ago, the Lord's help came to me in a dream. I was curled around a water toy, pulled by a speedboat I could not see, hanging on as my entire body bounced through rushing rapids. A divine hand protected me from the turbulence, but only if I kept my head down, focused on the task of clinging. Focus on the task at hand and let Him navigate. With God, nothing is impossible!

Our little ship is moving to a new port this summer. The logistical details are stretching my practiced "curl" into a dizzy, duty-driven tizzy. When I had my vision, the storms were not of my choosing and beyond my control. This time, the storms affecting my navigation feel self-inflicted. After all, it's a good move, to a better job!

Whether the storms are chosen or inflicted, mild or catastrophic, God's help is crucial to our interior balance. An "even keel" is a gift, not an achievement.

Edith Stein was teaching in a girl's school when she began giving lectures on Catholic education. Frail and somber, she lacked the oratorical heft of her male counterparts. Often, she was introduced with apologies for her plain, juvenile appearance. But her comments were electrifyingly original!

Soon, her calendar was full, and newspapers published her speeches. Back at the school, however, she calmly graded exercise books and kept to her quiet routines of prayer and late nights preparing philosophical treatises.

Her 1932 speech in Salzburg secured her fame, and she dominated discussion at an academic conference in Paris. Thanks to the Nazis' rising influence, her career prospects ended and she entered the cloister in 1933. Imagine the shock of the sisters at the time of her clothing ceremony, when flowers and visitors poured in from across Europe! They had no inkling of the worldly success of Sr. Teresa Benedicta.

St. Teresa of Avila said, "All things pass; God never changes." As the waves hit the boat, I remind myself to reach for the Anchor just as the speed starts to pull me under the waves. Even on good days, when I'm tempted to look out across the water and admire the crests of the waves before they hit me full force, I know better.

"I can do all things through Him who strengthens me," reads Philippians 4:13. Amen. With Jesus in charge, this ship of fools will safely get to the new port, and we shall glorify Him who sent us by focusing on the tasks at hand.

Bible Study: Edna, Sarah and Anna - The Women of the Book of Tobit

Tobit 7:13-17

Then he called his daughter Sarah, and taking her by the hand he gave her to Tobias to be his wife, saying, "Here she is; take her according to the law of Moses, and take her with you to your father." And he blessed them.

Next he called his wife Edna, and took a scroll and wrote out the contract; and they set their seals to it. Then they began to eat.

And Raguel called his wife Edna and said to her, "Sister, make up the other room, and take her into it." So she did as he said, and took her there; and the girl began to weep. But the mother comforted her daughter in her tears, and said to her, "Be brave, my child; the Lord of heaven and earth grant you joy in place of this sorrow of yours. Be brave, my daughter."

Tobit 11:9-15

Then Anna ran to meet them, and embraced her son, and said to him, "I have seen you, my child; now I am ready to die." And they both wept. Tobit started toward the door, and stumbled. But his son ran to him and took hold of his father, and he sprinkled the gall upon his father's eyes, saying, "Be of good cheer, father." And when his eyes began to smart, he rubbed them, and the white films scaled off from the corners of his eyes. Then he saw his son and embraced him, and he wept and said,

"Blessed art thou, O God, and blessed is thy name for ever, and blessed are all thy holy angels. For thou hast afflicted me, but thou hast had mercy upon me; here I see my son Tobias!" And his son went in rejoicing, and he reported to his father the great things that had happened to him in Media."

(Revised Standard Version)

Context: The book of Tobit is a morality tale intended to help the faithful answer the question, "Why do the just suffer?" Tobit honors the traditional Mosaic law, even as an exile in Ninevah. Yet, he becomes blind and loses everything although remaining ritually pure. Despondent, he even accuses his wife Anna of stealing, and asks God for death and deliverance from misfortune.

Similarly suicidal, Sarah's SEVEN husbands died on sequential honeymoons. (Banish your tabloid suspicions– the demon did it!) Sarah and her mother don't cry from guilt, but because they expect the young stranger asking for her hand to suffer a similar fate. (Well, maybe the gossipy maids hurt, too.)

Tobias, son of Tobit, is the stranger sent to Sarah. He is accompanied by the angel Raphael and the entrails of a "magic fish," which can cast out demons. Tobit conquers the demon, wins the maiden's love and washes the blindness from his father's eyes. (Any resemblance to messianic imagery is entirely intended.)

The story also reflects two common myths of the ancient world, the "grateful dead," in which the deceased sends blessings upon his burial attendant, and the "dangerous bride," which may yet be extant. (Some men are still scared to get hitched, so I hear.)

Translation: Probably written around 200 BC, the oral tradition was common enough that Jesus probably heard it retold over a holiday meal more than once. Written versions have been recovered in Greek, including a copy among the Dead Sea Scrolls. There are also scraps of it found in both Aramaic and Hebrew.

It's an engaging story, and the details included would have moved its hearers to both tears and laughter. They needed encouragement to follow the Lord's precepts in a land hostile to their values. So do we!

Vocabulary:

endogamy: This is the technical term for the practice of requiring persons to marry within their social and/or religious class. Rather than a limit on a maiden's freedom, it was seen as a protection for both her and the interests of the larger clan. The story of Tobit is an apologetic on endogamy, which was key to the survival of the Jewish identity in the diaspora.

gall: This refers to the contents of the gallbladder, which would have had quite the pungent aroma.

Do your tears matter? The women of the book of Tobit appear to have an overabundance of them. As misfortunes and humiliations mount, the women speak fewer and fewer words, and their tears of sorrow dominate the story. (In fact, their tears were evidence of their sanity, compared to the self-righteous advice and observations they were offered by their community!) Still, very few words are spoken, and their role in the drama seems so passive.

Or is it?

Anna, the wife of Tobit, was practical enough to get a job to support the family while Tobit was moaning about his troubles. He accuses her of stealing, and also discounts her tears when he sends their only son out to recover their lost treasure. Tobit was a straight arrow on the ritual purity front, but he wasn't exactly a tender spouse.

Edna weeps over Tobit's story of his father, and weeps with her daughter, and probably wept as her husband pre-emptively dug an eighth grave. Yet, the few words she says are full of the promises of God: "Be brave!" In a difficult situation, sometimes the most precious gift is a stable confidence in God's deliverance and empathetic tears.

The fathers may have done a good job preserving the doctrines of the faith in this family, but the mothers made God real to their lucky children, even and especially through their tears.

Discussion Questions:

1. What makes you cry? Are there different shades to tears? How do your closest friends and family react to tears? Would you change anything about the tears in your life?

2. Men and women react to stress very differently. Men tend to either pick fights or bottle it up, while women are more likely to "tend and befriend." There are actually hormonal reasons for these differences. How does this affect the power of faith to make a difference in times of crisis?

3. Are you cheering more for Anna or Edna? Why? Do you relate more to mother or to daughter?

Chapter Nine: Humility
Seeing with the Eyes of God

The ants of summer have arrived. I caught one in the second floor bathroom, and another by the basement television. (The subterranean ant looked better fed, nearer the cracker crumbs!) My youngest spent hours face to face with them on the patio. Then, smoosh!

If I wait long enough, Mother Nature will take care of my pest problem with frost. But I'm unwilling to share my abode for the summer, so I redirected them to the Raid ant "hotel." I'm just exercising my dominion over the plants and animals of the Kingdom. It's all biblically correct.

But contextually, I pause. Aren't I like an ant compared to my Lord? Doesn't he watch my every move, full of suspense? The analogy dies as fast as the ants in the "hotel."

Human beings are not animals, but creatures created in the image and likeness of God. And God isn't capricious, immobile with wonder one moment and smashing the wanderers the next. But my vision is rather limited, just like the ant. Do the shadows I fear resemble efficient housewives or tolerant toddlers, soul-smashing or spiritual succor?

In between the freshness of youth and the wisdom of old age, we often misjudge the magnitude of both mountains and molehills.

In April 1933, after losing her professorship at Munster, Edith Stein wrote a letter to Pope Pius XI, politely requesting he denounce the anti-Semitism of the ascendant Nazi regime. She never received a response.

The Vatican signed a concordat with the Third Reich in July 1933, the first vain attempt at negotiation with Hitler. Unintentionally, the Church only strengthened the Reich. The crimes of the Nazis largely were not widely known until after the war.

We are a human, fallible Church, individually and corporately. United in the mystery of Christ, our actions and inactions affect the entire body. It is possible to misjudge a situation in myriad ways. Humility is born of radical awareness of human weakness.

However, true humility is a vigorous virtue. Based on the Latin word *humilis,* it connotes a low position in a hierarchy. Thus, healthy humility acknowledges the Creator, in addition to intimacy with His creatures.

God has infinite mercy on us, especially when none of our options appear right. From the crucible of the Nazi occupation of Europe, many great leaders emerged, including Pope John Paul II. He lived long enough to see Nazism and Communism crushed, and a renewal of the Catholic Church itself in the Second Vatican Council.

Edith Stein could not avoid death. She believed that her death would be united to Jesus' redemptive death. She wasn't exalting herself, but humbly giving testimony to God's vision for her life.

May we always find inspiration in the humble circumstances of our worst challenges. God will find us there and exalt the lowly.

Bible Study: My Word Shall Not Return to Me Empty

Isaiah 55:6-13

Seek ye the Lord, while he may be found: call upon him, while he is near. Let the wicked forsake his way, and the unjust man his thoughts, and let him return to the Lord, and he will have mercy on him, and to our God: for he is bountiful to forgive. For my thoughts are not your thoughts: nor your ways my ways, saith the Lord. For as the heavens are exalted above the earth, so are my ways exalted above your ways, and my thoughts above your thoughts. And as the rain and the snow come down from heaven, and return no more thither, but soak the earth, and water it, and make it to spring, and give seed to the sower, and bread to the eater:

So shall my word be, which shall go forth from my mouth: it shall not return to me void, but it shall do whatsoever I please, and shall prosper in the things for which I sent it. For you shall go out with joy, and be led forth with peace: the mountains and the hills shall sing praise before you, and all the trees of the country shall clap their hands. Instead of the shrub, shall come up the fir tree, and instead of the nettle, shall come up the myrtle tree: and the Lord shall be named for an everlasting sign, that shall not be taken away.

Context: The book of Isaiah is divided by scholars into three sections. This section is supposed to have been composed by "deutero-Isaiah", a prophet writing in Isaiah's stead after the Babylonian exile. You are probably more familiar with the first chapters of Deutero-Isaiah, memorialized by Handel's Messiah: "Comfort ye...comfort ye, my people...Behold your God."

Deutero-Isaiah was relentlessly encouraging. He's writing to a dispirited people, devastated by the destruction of Jerusalem, and exiled by the Babylonians. The temple, the center of their religious beliefs, is gone. The need to repent is past; God's mercy awaits!

Translation: This biblical passage originally appeared in Hebrew. It was translated into Greek for Jews in the diaspora, called the Septuagint. Much later, St. Jerome translated the Septuagint into the Latin Vulgate, upon which many modern Bibles are based.

Vocabulary:

"Seek ye the LORD": This phrase was commonly used to call the faithful to the temple. With the temple destroyed, it was understood as an exhortation to find Him outside the temple.

my word: Deutero-Isaiah speaks in verse 11 of "my word" not like a message, but an event. Later Christian commentators would find here a prophecy of the Messiah, but for Israel, it acknowledges the nearness of God's saving hand.

void: Many other translations render this word as "empty," as it has the connotation of annihilation or purposelessness. God has a purpose for each of us.

My husband and children shudder when Christmas approaches, because all through Advent, I belt out impoverished attempts at the alto parts for Handel's Messiah. "The voice that crieth in the wilderness" isn't so much preparing the way of the Lord as caterwauling.

But I remind them that "my word shall not return to me void," says the Lord. It ranks on my list of top ten Bible verses. Nothing God creates lacks a purpose. We are each uniquely formed according to his purpose. Omnipotence means his purpose is already taking into account our weaknesses and failings. Each moment, He is creating new possibilities for us to participate in His saving plan for His glory. Even bad cantatas sung in bathrooms can be redeemed. Saith your God.

Discussion Questions:

1. God's ways are not always obvious to us. Talk about a time when God's purpose was revealed in a place and time that surprised you. Did this incident affect your faith?

2. There are often monotonous and depressing tasks and chores involved in both the workplace and the home. Does God have a purpose for this? Or is a cigar sometimes just a cigar?

3. "Let the unrighteous man forsake his thoughts," reminds Isaiah. Oh, those pesky thoughts. A multitude of sins begin in the unfettered thoughts that pepper my cognition. Is there a healthy way to tap into the thoughts of God? If you were to let God be your thought police, what thoughts would he censor? Why?

Chapter Ten: Readiness
Mistress of Her Own Castle

In the Principles of Women's Education, Edith Stein says, "She is mistress of this castle [the fortified soul] as the handmaid of her Lord...ready for him who was given to her as a visible sovereign..."

Are you the mistress of your castle? When my husband was in the Marines, he had a jaunty title for me: "CINC-house." (Pronounced "sink," CINC means "Commander in Chief.") He knew better than to make plans without consulting his commanding officer, at home or at work. I'm pretty intense.

Everyone, man or woman, has a visible sovereign to obey. Even those at the top of their profession— CEOs, popes and presidents— are not free to exercise their own selfish inclinations, but must serve the common good. Or risk losing their jobs through mutiny or revolution.

Everyone is a follower.

Even a job in an assembly line making widgets will have its share of twists, turns and creative problem solving. Machinery breaks down, co-workers quit, and new managers botch your supply lines. You've got to stay awake on the job.

Staying awake on the job comes with the territory at my house. The role of stay-at-home mother appealed to me in the beginning. I'd be the queen of my own universe. My tiara fit well until I realized that my little princess was actually my boss, and I was a rather bumbling handmaid.

Darn! Somebody else got to be the queen! (That used to happen to me at work, too!) Now that she can babysit and drive, I realize how much I've learned from her.

She helped me figure out the boundaries of my castle, the limits of my strengths and the reality of my weaknesses. Each child after she arrived only reinforced the point: I needed a King!

I'm a better "CINC-house" in partnership with my husband. He insists that I rest when I am tired, eat salad when I prefer licorice, and write essays even when I am discouraged. Often, he reminds me to keep my priorities straight when daily life bumps me around.

The crucial difference between a beloved "CINC-house" and a Stepford wife lies in the loving embrace of a vocation given by God and refined by mutual sacrifice. This holds true for the working mom as well. Management or labor, husband or hausfrau, we do our best teamwork when we seek to make others shine. Christians don't center their striving on power, but on virtue.

Obedience in this sense is not a blind following, but receptivity to the gifts of God in each moment, a readiness to mine the grace hidden in the details. Doing your duty implies drudgery in the modern lexicon. But for the handmaid of the Lord, doing your duty reveals a new freedom where treasure is found.

The Blessed Virgin is the queen of receptive hearts. Her silent presence in the background reassures me, especially in my weakest moments. That desperate "Hail Mary" matters. It carries the regal bearing of the mother of all our hopes.

My discouraging days as a secretary and as a mother were no less fruitful than my happy days. There were surprising treasures in all the tense moments of my life. Sometimes I was given painful self-knowledge, and many times I had insights that were useful later. I like the woman my demanding bosses and cranky toddlers helped me become.

The mistress of her castle is ready to be a treasure hunter for God. I may not be the queen, but I know where She lives. With practice, I'll be ready to follow her home when the Bridegroom beckons us.

Bible Study: Ten Virgins Bearing Lamps

Matthew 25:1-13

Then shall the kingdom of heaven be like to ten virgins, who taking their lamps went out to meet the bridegroom and the bride. And five of them were foolish, and five wise. But the five foolish, having taken their lamps, did not take oil with them: But the wise took oil in their vessels with the lamps. And the bridegroom tarrying, they all slumbered and slept.

And at midnight there was a cry made: Behold the bridegroom cometh, go ye forth to meet him. Then all those virgins arose and trimmed their lamps. And the foolish said to the wise: Give us of your oil, for our lamps are gone out. The wise answered, saying: Lest perhaps there be not enough for us and for you, go ye rather to them that sell, and buy for yourselves. Now whilst they went to buy, the bridegroom came: and they that were ready, went in with him to the marriage, and the door was shut.

But at last come also the other virgins, saying: Lord, Lord, open to us. But he answering said: Amen I say to you, I know you not. Watch ye therefore, because you know not the day nor the hour.

Context: Weddings in biblical times were arranged by the family patriarch. Once the betrothal was made, it was legally binding. The wedding took place when the bridegroom brought the bride home, which in some cases took as long as a year. So, weddings were akin to housewarmings. When the fiancé sent the word "ready," his espoused waited with ten of her closest female relations, her bridesmaids. The celebration began at night so all could enjoy the procession. The marriage was not physically consummated until after the long party. The celebration was more involved than our weddings.

Translation: This story probably was originally told in Aramaic, the Semitic language spoken by Jesus. Scholars are not sure who translated this parable into Greek, but it is mentioned by Ignatius of Antioch in the first century A.D.

Vocabulary:

Lamps: The lamp was really more like a torch. A rag soaked in oil was affixed to a stick. To keep the torch burning for a long while (some weddings lasted as long as a week), flasks of oil were needed.

Virgins: Most translations use the term virgins, including Jerome's Vulgate (Greek *parthenos;* Latin *virginis*). The purity of young maidens was assumed.

Wise/foolish: (Greek: *phronimos/moros*) Also given as prudence, Matthew contrasts the wise and the foolish elsewhere, and the difference can be found in good deeds. Here, the oil symbolizes good deeds.

Watch ye therefore: Rendered also "stay awake" or "be vigilant," it connotes the readiness to act that the nervous wedding participants know. How will that union of persons change us? Watch, and find out!

Brides usually choose close relatives and friends for their attendants. It's an honor to be asked. Still, potential bridesmaids might justly why they ought to care about the needs of "bridezilla." A wedding is not just a perfect day for a princess, but the serious beginning to a new way of life. Christian discipleship is similarly radical.

This parable highlights the joy we ought to reserve for our final union with God, and the preparation for that union that begins with our relationship to the bride. While Protestants are not so sure, I am convinced that this parable has a single Bride (Mary), to whom we cleave as we wait for Jesus (the bridegroom) to bring us back to that home He has prepared for us.

In the ebb and flow of family and close friends, we work out our salvation. No one is unaffected by our sins while we wait. Waiting with Mary for Jesus, we will not have to worry about the baubles on the banquet tables, but whether our hearts are adorned properly and lit with the oil of good deeds done for love.

Discussion Questions:

1. Are you, or were you, bridezilla? Or do you know a bridezilla? What's the cure?

2. As Mary's attendant, do you feel more like a distant cousin or a treasured friend? How could you get to know her better?

3. Do you worry about when Jesus will come in glory? Why? Or, why not?

Appendix A: A Proposed Daily Life for Women, by Edith Stein

(Excerpt from "Fundamental Principles of Women's Education," Essays on Woman, pp. 143-145.)

In the talk which I gave in November 1930 in Berndorf concerning the foundations of women's education, I tried to draw the picture of woman's soul as it would correspond to the eternal vocation of woman, and I termed its attributes as expansive, quiet, empty of self, warm and clear. Now I am asked to say something regarding how one might come to possess these qualities.

I believe that it is not a matter of a multiplicity of attributes which we can tackle and acquire individually; it is rather a single total condition of the soul, a condition which is envisaged here in these attributes from various aspects. We are not able to attain this condition by willing it; it must be effected through grace. What we can and must do is open ourselves to grace; that means to renounce our own will completely and to give it captive to the divine will, to lay our whole soul, ready for reception and formation, into God's hands. Becoming empty and still are closely connected. The soul is replenished by nature in so many ways that one thing always replaces another, and the soul is in constant agitation, often in tumult and uproar.

The duties and cares of the day ahead crowd about us when we awake in the morning (if they have not already dispelled our night's rest). Now arises the uneasy question: How can all this be accommodated in one day? When will I do this, when that? How shall I start on this and that? Thus agitated, we would like to run around and rush forth. We must then take the reins in hand and say, "Take it easy! Not any of this may touch me now. My first morning's hour belongs to the Lord. I will tackle the day's work which he charges me with, and He will give me the power to accomplish it."

So, I will go to the altar of God. Here it is not a question of my minute, petty affairs, but of the great offering of reconciliation. I may participate in that, purify myself and be made happy, and lay myself with all my doings and troubles along with the sacrifice on the altar. And when the Lord comes to me then in Holy Communion, then I may ask him, "Lord, what do you want of me?" (St. Teresa). And after quiet dialogue, I will go to that which I see as my next duty.

I will still be joyful when I enter into my day's work after this morning celebration: my soul will be empty of that which could assail and burden it, but it will be filled with holy joy, courage, and energy. Because my soul has left itself, and entered into the divine life, it has become great and expansive. Love burns in it like a composed flame which the Lord has enkindled, and which urges my soul to render love and to inflame love in others: "*flammescat igne caritas ardor proximos*" (an excerpt from the Latin hymn *Nunc Sancte Nobis Spiritus*, translated: "let charity be inflamed with fire and ardor enkindle our neighbors.") And it sees clearly the next part of the path before it; it does not see very far, but it knows that when it has arrived at that place where the horizon now intersects, a new vista will then be opened.

Now begins the day's work, perhaps the teaching profession—four or five hours, one after the other. That means giving our concentration there. We cannot achieve in each hour what we want, perhaps in none. We must contend with our own fatigue, unforeseen interruptions, shortcomings of the children, diverse vexations, indignities, anxieties. Or perhaps it is office work: give and take with disagreeable supervisors and colleagues, unfulfilled demands, unjust reproaches, human meanness, perhaps also distress of the most distinct kind.

It is the noon hour. We come home exhausted, shattered. New vexations possibly await there. Now where is the soul's morning freshness? The soul would like to seethe and storm again: indignation, chagrin, regret. And there is still so much to do until evening. Should we not immediately go to it? No, not before calm sets in at least for a moment.

Each one must know, or get to know, where and how she can find peace. The best way, when it is possible, is to shed all cares again for a short time before the Tabernacle. Whoever cannot do that, whoever also possibly requires bodily rest, should take a breathing space in her own room. And when no outer rest whatever is attainable, when there is no place in which to retreat, if pressing duties prohibit a quiet hour, then at least she must for a moment seal herself off inwardly against all other things and take refuge in the Lord. He is indeed there and can give us in a single moment what we need.

Thus, the remainder of the day will continue, perhaps in great fatigue and laboriousness, but in peace. And when night comes, and retrospect shows that everything was patchwork and much which one had planned left undone, when so many things rouse shame and regret, then take all as it is, lay it in God's hands, and offer it up to Him. In this way, we will be able to rest in Him, actually to rest and to begin the new day like a new life.

This is only a small indication how the day could take shape in order to make room for God's grace. Each individual will know best how this can be used in her particular circumstances. It could be further indicated how Sunday must be a great door through which celestial life can enter into everyday life, and strength for the work of the entire week, and how the great feasts, holidays and the seasons of Lent, lived through in the spirit of the Church, permit the soul to mature the more year to year to the eternal Sabbath rest.

It will be an essential duty of each individual to consider how she must shape her plan for daily and yearly living, according to her bent and to her respective circumstances of life, in order to make ready the way for the Lord. The exterior allotment must be different for each one, and it must also adjust resiliently to the change of circumstances in the course of time. But the psychic situation varies with individuals and with each individual in different times. As to the means which are suitable for bringing about union with the eternal, keeping it alive or also enlivening it anew—such as contemplation, spiritual reading, participation in the liturgy, popular services, etc.—these are not fruitful for each person and at all times. For example, contemplation cannot be practiced by all and always in the same way.

It is important in each case to find out the most efficacious way and to make it useful for oneself. It would be good to listen to expert advice in order to know what one lacks and this is especially so before one takes on variations from a tested arrangement.

Appendix B: An Edith Stein Bibliography

The Institute for Carmelite Studies has the most comprehensive selection of Edith Stein's works in English translations. Visit: https://www.icspublications.org/collections/edith-stein

An Edith Stein Daybook. (Templegate Publishers, 1994) Translated from the German by Susanne Batzdorff. Susanne Batzdorff is Edith Stein's niece. This slim volume includes one quote per day taken from Stein's work in the original German. Her translations of her aunt are uniformly excellent.

Aunt Edith: The Jewish Heritage of a Catholic Saint. (Templegate Publishers, 1994) by Susanne Batzdorff. This insightful account corrects numerous errors in other biographies, and gives a larger context for the life and work of Edith Stein.

Edith Stein: Selected Writings. (Templegate Publishers, 1990) Translated from the German by Susanne Batzdorff. This volume contains poems, hymns, and an account of her entry into Carmel.

Edith Stein: Her Life In Photos and Documents. (ICS Publications, 1999) by Maria Amata Neyer. A concise look at Stein by the Cologne Carmel archivist.

Essays on Woman. (ICS Publications, 1996) Translated from the German by Freda Mary Oben, Ph.D. This is the text from lectures that Dr. Stein delivered to Catholic educators in several venues from 1928 - 1932, prior to entering the Cologne Carmel.

Life in a Jewish Family. (ICS Publications, 1986, 2016) Translated from the German by Josephine Koeppel, O.C.D. This is Edith's autobiography of her early years and education, which she began in the months prior to her reception into the Cologne Carmel as a novice. She was anxious about the future of the Jews when Hitler came to power, and sought to show the patriotism and positive qualities of her Jewish family. She continued to work on the biography in Carmel, even after leaving Germany for Echt, Holland.

Self-Portrait in Letters. (ICS Publications, 1993) Translated from the German by Josephine Koeppel, O.C.D. The letters in this volume span her early days as a teaching assistant to Husserl up to her arrest and deportation by the Nazis in Echt, Holland. Her correspondents are friends and colleagues, as well as family members. It is a wonderful window into her daily life, and provides details about her spirituality.

Appendix C: Some Thoughts on Bible Studies

"Prayer should accompany the reading of Sacred Scripture, so that a dialogue takes place between God and man. For 'we speak to him when we pray; we listen to him when we read the divine oracles.'" (Catechism of the Catholic Church, 2653)

There is a tension between the spiritual and intellectual approach to reading the Bible that deserves a brief note. Over the past 200 years, both Christians and even non-Christians have engaged with the Sacred Scriptures using the "historical-critical method." They have many types of analysis exploring the oral tradition behind the Old Testament as well as the handwritten copies made over the centuries. The various translations of the scriptures from the original Hebrew and Greek into modern languages also have been explored. This is called "exegesis."

It is not against Catholic doctrine to do "exegesis." The Second Vatican Council document on Scripture, The Word of God, *Dei Verbum,* states:

> *"To search out the intention of the sacred writers, attention should be given, among other things, to "literary forms." For truth is set forth and expressed differently in texts which are variously historical, prophetic, poetic, or of other forms of discourse. The interpreter must investigate what meaning the sacred writer intended to express and actually expressed in particular circumstances by using contemporary literary forms in accordance with the situation of his own time and culture. For the correct understanding of what the sacred author wanted to assert, due attention must be paid to the customary and*

characteristic styles of feeling, speaking and narrating which prevailed at the time of the sacred writer, and to the patterns men normally employed at that period in their everyday dealings with one another." (Dei Verbum 12)

At the same time, we acknowledge that exegesis by some scholars has actively sought to deter Christians from faith, and to present false teachings. Faithful Christians have rightly questioned the use of exegesis, when it leads to doubt and disunity.

The skepticism of some scholars about the One, Holy, Catholic and Apostolic Faith should not stop us from learning as much as we can to understand Sacred Scripture. We are not spiritual orphans – we have a Church dedicated to the truth. The primary point of reading the Bible, for us as Christians, is to know, love and serve God. Thus, the main purpose of Bible study is to deepen our faith.

The Bible studies found in *My Secret is Mine* Newsletter begin with some notes on the context, translation and vocabulary of the scripture passage, and the meditation is deliberately brief and leads to questions. Our sole aim is to provide interesting and relevant information that we hope will spark creative and inspiring discussions in a group setting. We sincerely seek to love Jesus more, each and every day.

The team at *My Secret is Mine* encourages you to put Jesus first. To the extent that our Bible studies are helpful, you will know them by their fruits (Matthew 7:16). And to the extent that knowing the "exegetical" details only obscures God's love for you, we encourage you and your study group to simply focus on the Word of God.

"All scripture, inspired of God, is profitable to teach, to reprove, to correct, to instruct in justice, that the man of God may be perfect, furnished to every good work." (2 Tim. 3:16-17)

A Prayer Before Reading Scripture

Spirit of wisdom, enlighten us to read your Word with the intention of both love and understanding, that we might do God's will. Help us to remember the Word as an inspiration to charity and justice. Unite our hearts with Your heart, that we might attain greater union with You. And, with Your grace, may our study benefit the souls of others with whom we share what You wish us to learn. Amen.

(based on a similar prayer by Fr. John Hardon, S.J.)

Appendix D: Discussion Questions for Groups

This volume was prepared with groups of women in mind. The questions below can be used with each chapter to get the conversation started.

1. Define the virtue in your own words. Think of an example of someone practicing the virtue from your personal experience, or, of NOT practicing the virtue and the consequences you observed of its presence or absence.

2. The disparity between the ideal and the real can sometimes frustrate us, especially if we feel that the ideal is too far from our daily experience. Does this virtue seem far off to you? How could our local parish help women to develop this virtue? What things are happening in your local parish that might interfere with acquiring this virtue?

3. The gifts of God are unique for each woman. Some virtues come more easily to habitual practice than others. Help one another. Is it possible to pray for the attainment of intermediate steps toward the fullness of this virtue in your life? What would a minor step look like for you?

4. Mary is the queen of all the virtues. In her Magnificat, she sings of her unworthiness, and yet she allowed God to transform her into the Mother of God. How might this virtue change your perception of yourself and your own holiness? What is possible for you, in God's eyes?

5. What scriptures remind you of this virtue? Perhaps you know a favorite quote, a novel or a poem that speaks to this virtue? (Or use the suggested Bible study or book review from *My Secret is Mine* newsletter.

My Secret is Mine
spirituality for Catholic women

FREE: *www.mysecretismine.com*

All of the content in this book originally appeared in *My Secret is Mine* newsletter.

"*Secretum meum mihi*," (It's Latin for "my secret is mine.") was Edith Stein's cryptic response when her best friend asked why she became a Catholic in 1922. Edith Stein became a Carmelite nun in 1934, but was killed at Auschwitz by the Nazis due to her Jewish ancestry. She is our patroness at *MY SECRET IS MINE*.

Don't you have a secret too?

At work, you never mention faith for fear of being misunderstood.

At church, you never mention your work because no one asks.

And family challenges are often too personal to mention to the church ladies.

Friends and family have a rightful place in our hearts, but we often feel inadequate to meet their needs. The daily pace never slows. Even though it has been a century since Edith converted, women of faith still struggle to be taken seriously.

MY SECRET IS MINE Newsletter publishes a monthly newsletter for Catholic women:

- Essays on themes like male/female cooperation, the dignity of women and the feminine call to prophecy.
- Inspirational interviews with Catholic women whose faith in Jesus has transformed their lives.
- Stories of real women throughout history who witnessed to the Messiah.
- Book reviews of novels (old and new) with female characters who challenge our self-understanding.
- Bible studies with context, translation notes from Greek and Hebrew, and historical insights from reputable scholars.
- Prayer intentions on a monthly theme with links to more context in real life.
- And thought-provoking quotations and insights to share with your friends and family.

Visit mysecretismine.com to sign up for the newsletter!

Also by Kristen West McGuire

My Secret is Mine
The Essential Woman
Holy Helpmates: Successful Male Female Partnerships Through the
Ages

Standalone
The Glory to be Revealed in You: A Spiritual Companion to Pregnancy

Watch for more at www.kristenwestmcguire.com.

About the Author

Kristen *West* McGuire is the founder of Secretum Meum Mihi Press. A graduate of Georgetown University and Wesley Theological Seminary, she lives in the Lowcountry of South Carolina with her husband, a retired Marine. They have eight adult children and three wonderful grandchildren.

Read more at www.kristenwestmcguire.com.

About the Publisher

Secretum Meum Mihi Press publishes of spirituality resources content (books, newsletters, podcasts and website) for Catholic women. *Secretum Meum Mihi* is Latin for "My secret is mine," which was St. Edith Stein's response when questioned about her conversion to the Catholic faith in 1922. The flagship newsletter (www.MySecretisMine.com) includes interviews, book reviews, bible studies, prayer intentions, historical sketches and themed essays in a series. Books are based on the newsletter and suitable for parish adult study groups.

Read more at https://www.secretummeummihipress.com.